TOM JONES and  as students at the University of Texas. Their first collaboration was for a campus production, *Hipsy-Boo*. Later they collaborated on the score and Jones wrote the original story for a musical, *Time Staggers On*. After a sojourn in the Army during which they wrote songs by mail, they came to New York and began writing songs and revue material for Julius Monk's Upstairs-at-the-Downstairs shows. THE FANTASTICKS began as a one-act play for Barnard College, produced on August 3, 1959. The full-length version opened May 3, 1960 at New York City's Sullivan Street Playhouse. Since then, the two have written a short musical film and the successful Broadway musicals 110 IN THE SHADE, I DO! I DO!, and CELEBRATION.

THE FANTASTICKS

**Book and Lyrics by
Tom Jones**

**Music by
Harvey Schmidt**

Suggested by a play
LES ROMANESQUES
by Edmund Rostand·

 A BARD BOOK/PUBLISHED BY AVON BOOKS

AVON BOOKS
A division of
The Hearst Corporation
1790 Broadway
New York, New York 10019

First Printing, May, 1968

BARD TRADEMARK REG. U. S. PAT. OFF. AND
OTHER COUNTRIES, REGISTERED TRADEMARK—
MARCA REGISTRADA, HECHO EN WINNIPEG, CANADA

Printed in Canada

UNV   20   19   18   17   16   15   14   13   12   11

For B. Iden Payne

Original Cast

THE FANTASTICKS was first presented by Lore Noto at the Sullivan Street Playhouse, New York City, on May 3rd, 1960, with the following cast:

THE MUTE............Richard Stauffer

EL GALLO...............Jerry Orbach

LUISA...................Rita Gardner

MATT.................Kenneth Nelson

HUCKLEBEE ....William Larson

BELLAMY..............Hugh Thomas

HENRY.................Thomas Bruce

MORTIMER............George Curley

THE HANDYMAN........Jay Hampton

* * *

THE PIANIST..............Julian Stein
THE HARPIST..........Beverly Mann

Directed by WORD BAKER
Musical Director and Arrangements by
JULIAN STEIN
Production designed by ED WITTSTEIN

Associate Producers
SHELLY BARON, DOROTHY OLIM,
ROBERT ALAN GOLD

Musical Numbers

THE FANTASTICKS

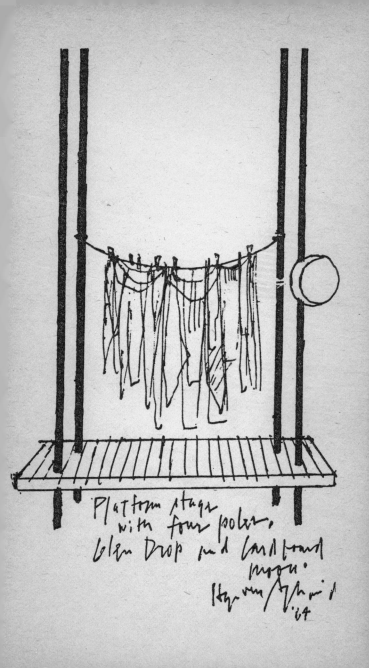

Platform stage
with four poles.
Glen Drop and Cardboard
moon.

Stephen Tylord
'64

ACT I

This play should be played on a platform. There is no scenery, but occasionally a stick may be held up to represent a wall. Or a cardboard moon may be hung upon a pole to indicate that it's night. When the audience enters the auditorium, the platform is clearly in sight, and there is a tattered drape across the front of it upon which is lettered "The Fantasticks."

During the Overture, the members of the Company arrive and prepare to do the play. They take down the lettered drape, set out the Prop Box, and put the finishing touches on their costumes. When the music is over, they take their places and wait while the Narrator (El Gallo) sings to the audience.

El G:
Sings.

Try to remember the kind of September
When life was slow and oh, so mellow.
Try to remember the kind of September
When grass was green and grain was yellow.
Try to remember the kind of September
When you were a tender and callow fellow.
Try to remember, and if you remember,
Then follow.

Luisa:
Follow, follow, follow, follow.

El G:

Try to remember when life was so tender
That no one wept except the willow.
Try to remember when life was so tender
That dreams were kept beside your pillow.
Try to remember when life was so tender
That love was an ember about to billow.
Try to remember, and if you remember,
Then follow.

Luisa:

Follow, follow, follow, follow.

Matt:

Follow, follow, follow, follow.

Fathers:

Follow, follow, follow, follow.

El G:

Deep in December, it's nice to remember,
Although you know the snow will follow.
Deep in December, it's nice to remember:
Without a hurt the heart is hollow.
Deep in December, it's nice to remember
The fire of September that made us mellow.
Deep in December, our hearts should remember,
And follow.

Speaks to audience.

Let me tell you a few things you may want to know
Before we begin the play.
First of all, the characters:

A boy; A girl; Two fathers;
And a wall.
Anything else that's needed
We can get from out this box.

MUTE displays Prop Box.

It's hard to know which is most important,
Or how it all began.
The Boy was born.
The Girl was born.
They grew up, quickly.
Went to school,
Became shy,
(In their own ways and for different reasons),
Read Romances,
Studied cloud formations in the lazy afternoon,
And instead of reading textbooks,
Tried to memorize the moon.
And when the girl was fifteen
(She was younger than the boy),
She began to notice something strange.
Her ugly duckling features
Had undergone a change.
In short, she was growing pretty;
For the first time in her whole life—pretty.
And the shock so stunned and thrilled her
That she became
Almost immediately
Incurably insane.
Observe:

Luisa:

The moon turns red on my birthday every year and
it always will until somebody saves me and takes
me back to my palace.

El G:

That is a typical remark.
The other symptoms vary.
She thinks that she's a princess;
That her name must be in French,
Or sometimes Eurasian,
Although she isn't sure what that is.

Luisa:

You see, no one can feel the way I feel
And have a father named Amos Babcock Bellomy.

El G:

She has a glue-paste necklace
Which she thinks is really real.

Luisa:

I found it in the attic
With my Mother's name inside;
It is my favourite possession.

El G:

It's her fancy.

Luisa:

It's my pride.

This morning a bird woke me up.
It was a lark or a peacock,

Or something like that.
Some strange sort of bird that I'd never heard.
And I said "hello."
And it vanished: flew away.
The very minute that I said "hello."
It was mysterious
So do you know what I did?
I went over to my mirror
And brushed my hair two hundred times
Without stopping.
And as I was brushing it,
My hair turned gold!
No, honestly! Gold!
And then red.
And then sort of a deep blue when the sun hit it.
I'm sixteen years old,
And every day something happens to me.
I don't know what to make of it.
When I get up in the morning to get dressed,
I can tell:
Something's different.
I like to touch my eyelids
Because they're never quite the same.

Oh! Oh! Oh!
I hug myself till my arms turn blue,
Then I close my eyes and cry and cry
Till the tears come down
And I taste them. Ah!
I love to taste my tears!

I am special.
I am special.
Please, God, please—
Don't let me be normal!

And, rapturously, SHE sings.

I'd like to swim in a clear blue stream
Where the water is icy cold;
Then go to town in a golden gown,
And have my fortune told.
Just once.
Just once.
Just once before I'm old.

I'd like to be—not evil,
But a little worldly wise.
To be the kind of girl designed
To be kissed upon the eyes.
I'd like to dance till two o'clock,
Or sometimes dance till dawn,
Or if the band could stand it,
Just go on and on and on!
Just once.
Just once.
Before the chance is gone!

I'd like to waste a week or two,
And never do a chore.
To wear my hair unfastened
So it billows to the floor.
To do the things I've dreamed about

20

But never done before!
Perhaps I'm bad, or wild, or mad,
With lots of grief in store,
But I want much more than keeping house!
Much more!
Much more!
Much more!

El G:
Good.
And now the boy.
His story may be a wee bit briefer,
Because it's pretty much the same.

Matt:
There is this girl.

El G:
That is the essence.

Matt:
There is this girl.

El G:
I warn you: it may be monotonous.

Matt:
There is this girl.
I'm nearly twenty years old.
I've studied Biology.
I've had an education.
I've been inside a lab:
Dissected violets.
I know the way things are.

I'm grown-up; stable;
Willing to conform.
I'm beyond such foolish notions,
And yet—in spite of my knowledge—
There is this girl.
She makes me young again, and foolish,
And with her I perform the impossible:
I defy Biology!
And achieve ignorance!
There are no other ears but hers to hear
the explosion of my soul! There are no other eyes
but hers to make me wise, and despite what they
say of species, there is not one plant or animal or
any growing thing that is made quite the same as
she is. It's stupid, of course, I know it. And im-
mensely undignified, but I do love her!

El G:

Look! There is the wall their fathers built between
their houses.

MUTE holds up stick.

Matt:

They built it ages ago last month when I came
home from school. Poor fools, they built it to keep
us apart. Maybe she's there now. I hope so—I'll
see. . . . I don't know what to call her. She's too
vibrant for a name. What shall I call her? Juliet?

Luisa:

Yes, dear!

22

Matt:
Helena?

Luisa:
Yes, dear!

Matt:
And Cassandra. And Cleopatra. And Beatrice. And also Guinevere?

Luisa:
What, dear?

Matt:
I think she's there.
Can you hear me?

Luisa:
Barely.

Matt:
I've been speaking of you.

Luisa:
To whom?

Matt:
To them—I told them that if someone were to ask me to describe you I would be utterly and totally speechless, except to say perhaps that you are Polaris or the inside of a leaf.

Luisa:
Speak a little louder.

Matt:
Sings.
I love you!

SHE swoons.

Matt:
Singing vigorously.
If I were in the desert deep in sand, and
The sun was burning like a hot pomegranate:
Walking through a nightmare in the heart of
A summer day, until my mind was parch-ed!
Then you are water!
Cool clear water!
A refreshing glass of water!

Luisa:
What, dear?

Matt:
Water!

SHE swoons.

Matt:
Sings.
Love! You are love!
Better far than a metaphor
Can ever ever be.
Love! You are love!
My mystery—of love!

If the world was like an iceberg,
And everything was frozen,

And tears turned into icicles in the eye!
And snow came pouring—sleet and ice—
Came stabbing like a knife!
Then you are heat!
A fire alive with heat!
A flame that thaws the iceberg with its heat!

Luisa:
Repeat.

Matt:
You are heat!

SHE swoons; then revives immediately to join him in song.

Love! You are love! (I am love!)
Better far than a metaphor
Can ever ever be.
Love! You are love! (I am love!)
My mystery—(his mystery) of love!

You are Polaris, the one trustworthy star!
You are! (I am!) You are! (I am!)
You are September, a special mystery
To me! (To he!) To me! (To he!)
You are Sunlight! Moonlight!
Mountains! Valleys!
The microscopic inside of a leaf!
My joy! My grief!
My star! My leaf!
Oh—

Both:

Love! You are love! (I am love!)
Better far than a metaphor
Can ever ever be!
Love! You are love! (I am love!)
My mystery—(his mystery)
Of love!

And THEY reach over the top of the stick, and embrace.

Luisa:

Matt!

Matt:

Luisa!

Luisa:

Shh. Be careful.
I thought I heard a sound.

Matt:

But you're trembling!

Luisa:

My father loves to spy.

Matt:

I know; I know.
I had to climb out through a window.
My father locked my room.

Luisa:

Oh God, be careful!
Suppose you were to fall!

Matt:
It's on the ground floor.

Luisa:
Oh.

Matt:
Still, the window's very small.
I could get stuck.

Luisa:
This is madness, isn't it?

Matt:
Yes, it's absolutely mad!

Luisa:
And also very wicked?

Matt:
Yes.

Luisa:
I'm glad.

Matt:
My father would be furious if he knew.

Luisa:
Listen, I have had a vision.

Matt:
Of disaster?

Luisa:
No. Of azaleas.

I dreamed I was picking azaleas.
When all at once, this Duke—
Oh, he was very old,
I'd say he was nearly forty.
But attractive.
And very evil.

Matt:

I hate him!

Luisa:

And he had a retinue of scoundrels,
And they were hiding behind the rhododendrons,
And then, all at once,
As I picked an azalea—
He lept out!

Matt:

God, I hate him!

Luisa:

In my vision, how I struggled.
Like the Rape of the Sabine Women!
I cried "help."

Matt:

And I was nearby!

Luisa:

Yes. You come rushing to the rescue.
And, single-handed, you fight all his men,
And win—

Matt:
And then—

Luisa:
Celebration!

Matt:
Fireworks!

Luisa:
Fiesta!

Matt:
Laughter!

Luisa:
Our fathers give in!

Matt:
We live happily ever after!

Luisa:
There's no reason in the world why it can't happen exactly like that.

Suddenly SHE stiffens.

Someone's coming!

Matt:
It's my father.

Luisa:
Kiss me!

THEY kiss as MUSIC begins and HUCKLEBEE comes in with pruning shears and prunes away at a massive imaginary plant.

29

Huck:

Too much moisture!

To audience.

There are a great many things I could tell you about myself. I was once in the Navy; that's where I learned Horticulture. Yes, I have been the world over. I've seen it all: mountain cactus, the century plant, Japanese Ivy. And exotic ports where bogwort was sold in the open market! I'm a man of experience and there is one thing that I've learned: Too much moisture is worse than none at all. Prune a plant. Avoid water. And go easy on manure. Moderation. That's the moral. Hmm. That's my son's foot.

Matt:

Hello, Father.

Huck:

What are you doing up in that tree?

Matt:

Reading verses.

Huck:

Curses.

Matt:

How's that?

Huck:

I offer a father's curses
To the kind of education
That makes our children fools.

I sent this boy to school—to college;
And I hope you know what that costs.
Did he learn to dig a cesspool, no.
He's up there reading verse.
Why do I always find you
Standing beside that wall?

Matt:

I'm waiting for it to fall.
Besides, I like it.
I like its lovely texture,
And its pretty little eyes.

Huck:

Walls don't have eyes!

Matt:

Then what do you call this flower?

Luisa:

Sweet God, he's clever!

Huck:

Son, you are an ass. There you sit every day, reading verses, while who knows what our neighbor is up to on the other side of that wall. He's a villain. I'll not have it! I'll strip down those branches where an enemy could climb! I'll lime that wall with bottles! I'll jag it up with glass!

Luisa:
Ahh!

31

Huck:
What was that?

Matt:
Some broken willow—some little wounded bird.

Huck:
Maybe. But walls have ears even though they don't have eyes. I'll just take a look.

Starts to climb and then stops.

Ahh! There's that stiffness. The result of my Navy career. Here, son, you climb. You can see for me.

Matt:
All right, Father.

Huck:
What do you see?

Matt:
I love you.

Luisa:
I love you, too.

Huck:
What are you mumbling about? Get down from there if there's nothing to be seen! Down I say.

Matt:
I obey.

Huck:
You're an idiot. I've decided you need to be married. So I went shopping this morning and picked you out a wife.

Luisa:
   Ahh!

Huck:
   There's that sound again.

Matt:
   Anguished bird.

Huck:
   Weeping willow?
   It may be.
   But let's get back to business:
   Son, I've picked you out a pearl.

Matt:
   And if I prefer a diamond?

Huck:
   How dare you prefer a diamond
   When I've just offered you a pearl!

Matt:
   Listen carefully to what I have to say.
   Listen, Wall. And flowers. And willow, too.
   And wounded bird. And Father, you
   May as well listen too.
   I will not wed by your wisdom.
   I will not walk neatly into a church
   And contract out to prolongate my race.
   I will not go wedding in a too-tight suit
   Nor be witnessed when I take my bride.
   No!

Music as HE speaks.

I'll marry, when I marry,
In my own particular way;
And my bride shall dress in sunlight,
With rain for her wedding veil.
Out in the open,
With no one standing by.
No song except September
Being sung in the busy grass!
No sound except our heartbeats, roaring!
Like a flower alive with bees!
Without benefit of neighbor!
Without benefit of book!
Except perhaps her handprint
As she presses her hand in mine;
Except perhaps her imprint
As she gives me her golden hair;
In a field, while kneeling,
Being joined by the joy of life!
There!
In the air!
In the open!
That's how I plan to wive!

Huck:

Son, you need pruning. Come inside and write
SIMPLICITY two hundred times without stopping. Perhaps that will improve your style.

MATT and HUCKLEBEE exit. MUSIC as

BELLOMY enters on his side, carrying an enormous watering pail with a long spout.

Bell:

That's right, drink away. Open up your thirsty little mouths.

To audience.

I'm her father. And believe me, it isn't easy. Perhaps that's why I love vegetables. So dependable. You plant a radish, and you know what you're about. You don't get a turnip or a cabbage, no. Plant a turnip, get a turnip; plant a cabbage, get a cabbage. While with children—I thought I had planted a turnip or at worst perhaps an avocado: something remotely useful. I'm a merchant—I sell buttons. What need do I have for a rose?—There she is. Missy, you must go inside.

Luisa:

I've told you; I'm a princess.

Bell:

You're a button-maker's daughter. Now, go inside as you're told. Our enemy is beyond that wall. Up to something: I can feel it! Him and his no-good son. Look out, you've stepped in my peppers. That settles it. I'll put a fence here by this wall. A high fence, with barbed stickers! An arsenal of wire!

Luisa:

A fence is expensive, Papa.

Bell:
Expensive? Well, I'll build it myself. Go inside; do
as I tell you!
Is she gone?—Ha, yes—she's gone.

Yodels.

Oh lady le di le da loo!

*HE puts his hand to his ear and we hear in the dis-
tance an answering yodel. BELLOMY yips with
delight and rushes over to the bench as HUCKLE-
BEE does the same on his side. THEY scramble up
the bench and noisily embrace over the "wall."*

Bell:
Hucklebee!

Huck:
Bellomy!

Bell:
Neighbor!

Huck:
Friend!

Bell:
How's the gout?

Huck:
I barely notice. And your asthma?

Bell:
A trifle.

Coughs.

I endure it.

Huck:
Well, it's nearly settled.

Bell:
What is?

Huck:
The marriage. They're nearly ready. I hid in the bushes to listen. Oh, it's something; They're out of their minds with love!

Bell:
Hurray.

Huck:
My son—he is fantastic!

Bell:
My daughter is fantastic, too.
They're both of them mad.

Huck:
They are geese!

Bell:
It was a clever plan we had.
To build this wall.

Huck:
Yes. And to pretend to feud.

Bell:
Just think if they knew
That we wanted them wed.

Huck:
A pre-arranged marriage—

Bell:
They'd rather be dead!

MUSIC.

Huck:
Children!

Bell:
Lovers!

Huck:
Fantasticks!

Bell:
Geese!

Huck:
How clever we are.

Bell:
How crafty to know.

Huck:
To manipulate children,

Bell:
You merely say "no."

And THEY sing.

Ohhhhhhhh—
Dog's got to bark; a mule's got to bray.
Soldiers must fight and preachers must pray.
And children, I guess, must get their own way
The minute that you say no.

Why did the kids pour jam on the cat?
Raspberry jam all over the cat?
Why should the kids do something like that,
When all that we said was "No"?

Huck:
My son was once afraid to swim;
The water made him wince.
Until I said he mustn't swim;
'S been swimmin' ever since!

Both:
'S been swimmin' ever since!

Ohhhhhhhh—
Dog's got to bark; A mule's got to bray.
Soldiers must fight and preachers must pray.
And children, I guess, must get their own way
The minute that you say no.

Why did the kids put beans in their ears?
No one can hear with beans in their ears.
After a while the reason appears.
They did it 'cause we said "No."

Bell:
Your daughter brings a young man in,
Says 'Do you like him, Pa?'

Just tell her he's a fool and then,
You've got a son-in-law!

Both:
You've got a son-in-law!
Ohhhhhhhhhhhhhhh—
Sure as a June comes right after May!
Sure as the night comes right after day!
You can be sure the devil's to pay,
The minute that you say no.
Make sure you never say—
No!

Bell:
But there's one problem left.

Huck:
How to end the feud?

Bell:
Exactly; you guessed it.
We mustn't let them know.

Huck:
Oh no, if they knew—
We're finished.

Bell:
We're through.

Huck:
I think I've found the answer.
It's delicious. Very theatrical.

Bell:
Tell me.

Huck:
An abduction!

Bell:
Who's abducted?

Huck:
Your daughter.

Bell:
Who abducts her?

Huck:
A professional abductor.
I've hired the very man!

Enter EL GALLO, with a flourish.

El G:
Gentlemen, good evening.

Huck:
What the devil?

Bell:
Who are you?

El G:
I was sent for.
A maiden in distress.

Huck:
Of course, you are El Gallo.
HE pronounces it American—
Gal-oh.

El G:
HE pronounces it Spanish—
Gayo.

Huck:

Oh—si, si.

To BELLOMY.

See, this is what I was about to tell you. We hire this man to assist us. He starts to kidnap your daughter. My son runs in to save her. Then, a battle.

El G:

I allow the boy to defeat me . . .

Huck:

My son becomes a hero . . . and the feud is over forever.

Bell:

How much for such a drama?

El G:

That, Señor, depends.

Bell:

On what?

El G:

What else? The quality of the Rape.

Bell:

No.

HE starts to leave, but THEY catch him.

El G:

Forgive me. The attempted Rape. I know you prefer Abduction, but the proper word is Rape. It's short and businesslike.

Huck:
I heard you speak of Sabine Women.

Bell:
Well, it doesn't sound right to me!

El G:
It is though, I assure you.
As a matter of fact, it's standard.
The lovers meet in secret. And so forth.
A group of villains interrupt them. And so forth.
The boy fights off pirates, Indians, bandits.
The parents relent. Happy ending. And so forth.
All of it quite standard.

Bell:
What about the cost?

El G:
Cost goes by type. In your case, I think I would
recommend a "First Class."

Bell:
You mean we get a choice?

El G:
Yes, of course. With regular Union rates.

Sings.

Rape!
R-a-a-a-pe!
Raa-aa-aa-pe!
A pretty rape.
Such a pretty rape!

We've the obvious open schoolboy rape,
With little mandolins and perhaps a cape,
The rape by coach; it's little in request.
The rape by day; but the rape by night is best.

Just try to see it,
And you will soon agree, Señors,
Why invite regret,
When you can get the sort of rape
You'll never ever forget!

You can get the rape emphatic.
You can get the rape polite.
You can get the rape with Indians,
A truly charming sight.
You can get the rape on horseback,
They all say it's new and gay.
So you see the sort of rape
Depends on what you pay.
It depends on what you pay.

Huck:
The kids will love it.
It depends on what you—

Bell:
Pay!

Huck:
So why be stingy,
It depends on what you—

El G:
The spectacular rape,
With costumes ordered from the East.

Requires rehearsal
And takes a dozen men at least.
A couple of singers
And a string quartet.
A major production—requires a set.

Just try to see it,
And you will soon sí, sí, Señor,
Why invite regret,
When you can get the sort of rape
You'll never ever forget!

You can get the rape emphatic.
You can get the rape polite.
You can get the rape with Indians:
A truly charming sight!
You can get the rape on horseback,
They all say it's distingué!
So you see the sort of rape
Depends on what you pay.
It depends on what you pay.

Huck:
  So why be stingy.
  It depends on what you—

Bell:
  Pay, pay, pay!

Huck:
  The kids will love it;
  It depends on what you—

El G:
The comic rape!
Perhaps it's just a trifle too unique. (Ha ha)
Romantic rape.
Done while canoeing on a moonlit creek.
The Gothic rape!
I play Valkyrie on a bass bassoon!
The drunken rape!
It's done completely in a cheap saloon.
The rape Venetian—needs a blue lagoon.
The rape with moonlight—or without a moon.
Moonlight is expensive but it's in demand.
The military rape,
It's done with drummers and a band.
You understand?
It's very grand!
It's done with drums and a great big brass band!

EL GALLO and FATHERS dance.

Bell:
It's so Spanish; that's why I like it!

Huck:
I like it, too, Ai, yi, yi!

El G:
Just try to see it.

Bell:
I see it!

Huck:
I see it!

46

El G:

> And you will soon sí, sí, Señor.
> Why—invite regret,
> When you can get the sort of rape
> You'll never ever forget!

Fathers:

> We can get the rape
>   emphatic.
> We can get the rape
>   polite.
> We can get the rape
>   with Indians:
> A truly charming sight.
> We can get the rape on
>   horseback,
> They all say it's new
>   and gay.
> So you see the sort of
>   rape
> Depends on what you
>   pay.
> So you see the sort of
>   rape
> Depends on what you
>   pay.

El G:

> Oh, rape!
> Sweet rape.
> Oh, rape.
> Ah—rape—
> RA—AA—
> AA—AA—
> AA—PE!

All Three:

> Depends a lot
> On what you —

Huck:
Speaks.
I say they're only young once—
Let's order us a First Class!

All Three:
Sing.
Ra-aa-aa-pe!
Olé!

El G:
With pad and pencil.
One Rape First Class.

Bell:
With trimmings!

El G:
Makes note.
With trimmings. Now, let's see—is it to be a big affair, or intimate?

Bell:
We thought—just the children.

El G:
I mean afterwards, at the party.

Bell:
No. Just the immediate family.

El G:
No guests? Perhaps a gathering on the lawn?

Bell:
Too expensive. Just the immediate family will be enough.

El G:

As you wish. That means the orchestra can go home.

Still, big affairs are nice.

Huck:

Perhaps some other time.

El G:

All right then. You'd better go home and rehearse your parts.

Exit FATHERS.

La. Time is rushing. And a major production to do. I need actors—extra actors—to stage my elaborate Rape. But I'm not worried. Something will turn up. I can sense it in the air.

Drumbeat.

There—you hear? What did I tell you?

The MUTE opens the prop box and MORTIMER emerges, dressed in a loin cloth and a feather, and playing a drum. HE is followed at once by HENRY, an ancient actor down on his luck.

Henry:

Sir, the Players have arrived!

El G:

Señor, the Players are most welcome.

Henry:

Don't look at us like we are, sir. Please. Remove ten pounds of road dust from these aged wrinkled cheeks. See make-up caked, in glowing powder pink! Imagine a beard, full blown and blowing,

49

like the whiskers of a bear! And hair! Imagine hair.
In a box I've got all colors, so I beg you—imagine
hair!—And not these clothes. Oh no, no, no. Dear
God, not rags like any beggar has. But see me in a
doublet! Mortimer, fetch the doublet.

MORTIMER sheathes him in a worn-out doublet.

There—Imagine! It's torn; I know—forget it. It
vanishes under light. That's it! That's the whole
trick; try to see me under light! I recite. Say a cue.
You'll see. I'll know it. Go on. Say one. Try me.

El G:
"Friends, Romans, Countrymen."

Henry:
It's what?

El G:
"Friends, Romans, Countrymen."

Henry:
—Don't tell me. I can get it. Let's see. "Friends,
Romans, Countrymen."

MORTIMER whispers it to him.

Why yes! Of course! That's easy. Why didn't you
pick something hard?

Strikes a pose.

Friends, Romans, Countrymen—
Screw your courage to the sticking place!
And be not sick and pale with grief

50

That thou—her handmaidens—
Should be far more fair
Than she . . . is . . .
How's that?

El G:
Amazing.

Henry:
Try to see it under light. I assure you it's dazzling.
I'm Henry Albertson. Perhaps you recall my Hamlet?

El G:
Of course.

Henry:
Stunned.
You remember? Would you like to see the clippings?

El G:
Perhaps later.

Henry:
As you wish. I preserve them. Who knows—I may
write a book someday. This is Mortimer; he does
death scenes. He's been with me for forty years.
Want to see one? He's an expert. Mortimer, die for
the man.

MORTIMER dies.

You see! What did I tell you!—Now, down to
business. You need Players?

51

El G:

For a love scene. Have you done romantic drama?

Henry:

That sir, is my specialty. Have you never seen my Romeo?

El G:

I'm afraid not.

Henry:

Oh well, I have the clippings.

Starts to get them, but EL GALLO grabs him.

El G:

Henry, here's the path: We'll have these players play something like the abduction of the maiden before this lover—

Henry:

Catching the spirit.

And if he but blench!

El G:

We'll stand our ground. And fight until the lot of us is downed!

Henry:

Nobly done!

Mort:

Rising from the dead, and speaking with a very thick Cockney accent.

Where do you want me, 'Enry?

Henry:

Hm? Oh! Off left, Mortimer. Indians are always off left.

Mort:
Wot's my cue?

Henry:
I'll tell you when it's time.

Mort:
Righto.

And HE exits—off stage left.

Henry:
Calling out after him.
Don't forget, Mortimer: dress the stage, dress the
stage. Don't cluster up when you die.

To EL GALLO.

Well, that does it, I think. I imagine we'd better
hide.

El G:
Oh, I nearly forgot. I promised them moonlight.

*HE snaps his fingers and the MUTE hangs up the
moon.*

Henry:
Amazing!

El G:
Beautiful, eh? A lover's moon—
Go ahead, Henry. I'll be right there.

*HENRY eixts, and EL GALLO speaks to the audi-
ence as the MUTE mimes the sensations and the
words.*

You wonder how these things begin.
Well, this begins with a glen.
It begins with a Season, which,
For want of a better word,
We might as well call September.

MUSIC.

It begins with a forest where the woodchucks woo
And leaves wax green,
And vines entwine like lovers; try to see it:
Not with your eyes, for they are wise;
But see it with your ears:
The cool green breathing of the leaves.
And hear it with the inside of your hand:
The soundless sound of shadows flicking light.
Celebrate sensation.
Recall that secret place;
You've been there, you remember:
That special place where once—
Just once—in your crowded sunlit lifetime,
You hid away in shadows from the tyranny of time.
That spot beside the clover
Where someone's hand held your hand,
And love was sweeter than the berries,
Or the honey,
Or the stinging taste of mint.
It is September,
Before a rainfall—
A perfect time to be in love.

Enter MATT and LUISA.

Matt:
   Hello.

Luisa:
   Hello.
   My father is going to be very angry.

Matt:
   I know. So is mine.

Luisa:
   We've never been here at night.

Matt:
   No.

Luisa:
   It's different from the day.

Matt:
   Are you frightened?

Luisa:
   Yes; no.
   Brr. It's cold here. There's going to be a storm.

Matt:
   Would you like my jacket?

Luisa:
   No, thank you. Matt.

Matt:
   Yes?

Luisa:
   My hand is trembling.

Matt:
Don't be afraid. Please.

Luisa:
All right. I promise.
Thunder. LUISA rushes into MATT'S arms.

Matt:
There, there. It's all right.

Luisa:
Matt, take care of me. Teach me. I don't want to be awkward—or afraid. I love you, Matt. I want there to be a happy ending.

Matt:
I promise that there will be.
Kisses her.
Look.

Luisa:
What?

Matt:
Smiles.
My hand is trembling too.

Luisa:
Sings.
Hear how the wind begins to whisper.
See how the leaves go streaming by.
Smell how the velvet rain is falling,
Out where the fields are warm and dry.
Now is the time to run inside and stay.
Now is the time to find a hideaway—
Where we can stay.

Matt:

Soon it's gonna rain;
I can see it.
Soon it's gonna rain;
I can tell.
Soon it's gonna rain;
What are we gonna do?

Soon it's gonna rain;
I can feel it.
Soon it's gonna rain;
I can tell.
Soon it's gonna rain;
What'll we do with you?

We'll find four limbs of a tree.
We'll build four walls and a floor.
We'll bind it over with leaves.
Then duck inside to stay.

Then we'll let it rain;
We'll not feel it.
Then we'll let it rain;
Rain pell-mell.
And we'll not complain
If it never stops at all.
We'll live and love
Within our own four walls.

THEY talk now, as the MUSIC continues.

Would you like for me to show you around the castle?

Luisa:

Oh yes, please.

Matt:

The lookout tower. And the throne. And this, the
family pride and joy: the ballroom!

Luisa:

My, how grand.

Matt:

Princess.

Luisa:

Your highness.

*And THEY begin to dance—at first grand and
sweeping and then more and more tenderly as the
wind continues to swirl in. As the thunder rolls
again, MATT pulls her up on the platform and the
MUTE sprinkles them with paper rain.*

Matt:

We'll find four limbs of a tree.
We'll build four walls and a floor.
We'll bind it over with leaves,
Then duck inside to stay.

Both:

Then we'll let it rain;
We'll not feel it.
Then we'll let it rain;
Rain pell-mell.
And we'll not complain
If it never stops at all.

We'll live and love
Within our castle walls.

*At the end of the song, HENRY comes back in.
HE signals for the Audience to be quiet; then HE
speaks to the MUSICIANS.*

Henry:
Accelerando con molto!
*As the MUSIC begins for the Rape Ballet,
HENRY calls out "Swords" to the MUTE, who
rushes to the prop box and removes four wooden
sticks. Then HENRY calls out:*

Indians, ready?
Indians—Rape!

*And MORTIMER springs out of his hiding place.
HE snatches up the astonished LUISA right before
the eyes of the equally astonished MATT and starts
to carry her out Right. But HENRY, in a fury, in-
terrupts him.*

Henry:
No, no. Off left, Damn it!

Mort:
All right, all right.

*And HE faithfully totes her left. By now MATT
has recovered himself sufficiently to interrupt their
progress. HE struggles with MORTIMER as
HENRY grabs up the disentangled LUISA. MOR-
TIMER rushes over. HE and HENRY pick up*

the girl and try to carry her out—each in a different direction, of course. The MUTE hands MATT the drum sticks to MORTIMER's Indian Drum, and MATT floors both the old actors with a mighty whop of the sticks. LUISA rushes up to her protector as HENRY struggles to his feet.

Henry:
Feeling his head.

"A touch, A touch. I do confess it."

Now, the moment is ripe for the big scene. HENRY rushes to the side and yells out: "Cavalry!" which is the cue for EL GALLO to enter into the fray. EL GALLO sweeps on with a flourish. The MUTE supplies both HE and MATT with wood swords and THEY begin to fight. During the midst of their battle, EL GALLO is thrown to the side and HENRY catches him and yells out: "Once more, dear friends, into the breach!" At this signal the MUTE supplies HENRY and MORTIMER with stick swords and all three "villains" sword-fight our young hero at once—not at all unlike the Douglas Fairbanks movies of the good old days. THEY advance. THEY retreat. Then—with a mighty push, MATT sends them all sprawling to the floor. MORTIMER rises—rushes forward— is killed dramatically. HENRY rises—and as HE charges, cries out—

Henry:
"God for Harry, England, and Saint Geo - - ough!"

The last word becomes a vivid "ouch" as HE is wounded and falls dead. Only EL GALLO is left now. HE and MATT square off and have at it. For a while it's nip and tuck as the two men fight up and down upon the platform, and clash together every once in a while so that THEY stand gritting, tooth to tooth, across the criss-crossed sabers. In the end, EL GALLO allows himself to be defeated and HE dies in so grand a manner that even MOR-TIMER cannot resist a look of admiration. EL GALLO dies like a diva in the opera, rising again and again from the floor, to give one last dramatic, agonized twitch.

When EL GALLO goes down for the last time, the MUSIC becomes jolly and triumphant. The young lovers rush upon the little platform and embrace in a pretty tableau. The FATHERS rush in too. And embrace too. And get upon the plat-form to finish off the "Living Statues" type of tableau.

All these speeches are over MUSIC.

Luisa:
Matt!

Matt:
Luisa!

Huck:
Son!

Bell:
Daughter!

Huck:

To BELL.

Neighbor!

Bell:

To HUCK.

Friend!

Luisa:

To the world.

I always knew there would be a happy ending!

The MUSIC suddenly stops. THEY all freeze as EL GALLO rises, rather painfully, from the dead.

El G:

Feeling his back.

I think I pulled something.

Mort:

Oh, you get a bit sore at first; dying like that. It's not the easiest thing in the business. But I like it. I've been dying for forty years, ever since I was a boy. Ah, you should have seen me in those days. I could die off a twenty foot cliff backwards! People used to cry out: "Die again, Mortimer—die again!" But of course I never did.

El G:

Well, Henry. Are you off now?

Henry:

Yes. Going somewhere. There's not much left to the old Company anymore—just Mortimer and me. But we make out. I recite Shakespeare. Mortimer dies. There's usually an audience somewhere. Oh—here's your moon.

El G:

Thank you—"Good night, Sweet Prince."

Henry:

After first pushing MORTIMER out of "his" light.

"And flights of angels sing thee to thy rest—Why doth the drum come hither?" Remember, Mortimer, there are no small actors—only small parts.

HENRY and MORTIMER step back into the prop box, and—just before HE disappears under the lid, HENRY looks out to the audience and speaks.

Remember me—in light!

And HE is gone. EL GALLO looks at the LOVERS and their PARENTS still frozen on the stage. Like a choral conductor, HE conducts them in the short contrapuntal selection called "HAPPY ENDING."

El G:

When THEY are through singing.
Very pretty, eh?
Worthy of Watteau.
A group of living statues:
What do they call it?
A tableau.
Hmmm.
I wonder if they can hold it.

They'll try to, I suppose.
And yet it won't be easy
To hold such a pretty pose.
We'll see.
We'll leave them for a little
Then we'll see.

EL GALLO and the MUTE hang the "FAN-TASTICKS" drape, in front of the actors.

Act One is over.
It's the Intermission now.

ACT II

EL GALLO re-enters, carrying the moon. HE nods
to the MUTE, who undoes the flap and lowers the
curtain on the little platform stage. The PARENTS
and the LOVERS are still there, poised in their
pretty tableau. But THEY seem less graceful now,
as if there were some pain involved in holding the
pose so long.

El G:
Their moon was cardboard, fragile.
It was very apt to fray,
And what was last night scenic
May seem cynic by today.
The play's not done.
Oh no—not quite,
For life never ends in the moonlit night;
And despite what pretty poets say,
The night is only half the day.

So we would like to truly finish
What was foolishly begun.
For the story is not ended
And the play is never done
Until we've all of us been burned a bit
And burnished by—the sun!

HE reverses the moon. On the other side is the sun.
HE throws it into the air, making daylight. And
one by one, the PARENTS and the CHILDREN
begin to break from the tableau. Their eyes sting in
the hot red sun. The music underneath is sour—
disgruntled.

Huck:
It's hot.

Bell:
What?

Huck:
Hot!

Bell:
Oh. Sssss—

Luisa:
And now we can meet in the sunlight.

Matt:
And now there is no more wall.

Luisa:
Aren't we happy?

Matt:
Yes. Aren't we.

Chord.

Luisa:
He looks different in the sunlight.

Matt:
I'm not ready to get married yet.

Luisa:
I thought he was taller, somehow.

Matt:
When you get right down to it, she's only the girl next door.

Chord.

Huck:
  Neighbor.

Bell:
  Friend.

Huck:
  In-law.

Bell:
  Ugh.
  Chord.

Huck:
  This is what we've always wanted.
  Our gardens are one.

Bell:
  We're merged.

Huck:
  Related.

Bell:
  Amalga-

Huck:
  Mated.

Bell:
  Well.

  Chord! As MATT and LUISA step down off the platform, HUCK gets his clippers and BELL his watering pail.

Luisa:
  What shall we do today?

Matt:
Whatever you say.

Luisa:
And tomorrow?

Matt:
The same!

Chord.

I wonder where that road goes.

Luisa:
I'd like to swim in a clear blue stream—

Chord.

Huck:
Water, water, water!

Bell:
What did you say?

Huck:
I said, Water, Water, Water!

Bell:
Clip, Clip, Clip!

Huck:
What?

Bell:
You're clipping my kumquat!

Huck:
Rot!

The music for the quartet has begun as the FOUR PRINCIPALS pace back and forth, MATT and

LUISA eating plums which the MUTE has given to them.

Luisa:
This plum is too ripe!

Matt:
Sorry.

Music.

Please don't watch me while I'm eating.

Luisa:
Sorry.

Music.

Huck:
You're about to drown that magnolia!

Bell:
Sorry!

Music.

You're—standing—in—my—KUMQUAT!

Huck:
SORRY!

And the quartet begins, first as solos, and then as a round.

Luisa:
Take away the golden moonbeam.
Take away the tinsel sky.
What at night seems oh so scenic,
May be cynic by and by.

Matt:

Take away the painted sunset.
Take away the blue lagoon.
What at night seems oh so scenic,
May be cynic much too soon.

Bell:

Take away the secret meetings.
Take away the chance to fight.
What at night seems oh so scenic
May be cynic in the light.

Huck:

Take away the sense of drama.
Take away the puppet play.
What at night seems oh so scenic
May be cynic by today.

All:

So take it away and paint it up right!
Yes, take it away and decorate it!
So take it away, that sun is too bright!
I say that it really is a pity;
It used to be so pretty.

And now the round, ending with:

Matt:

Spoken.

This plum is too ripe!

All:
SORRY!

Huck:

When the music is over.

I was a fool to tear down that wall.

Bell:
So was I. I hate people tromping in my garden!

Luisa:
Please. No fighting.
You see, I come like Cassandra
With a figleaf in my hand.

Bell:
It was Minerva.

Huck:
And that's a plum.

Luisa:
Well!

Matt:
Don't mind them, dear.
I think they're jealous.

Huck:
Jealous?

Matt:
Of us. Of our passion—and our youth.

Bell:
Fantastic!

Matt:
You see—they are jealous!

Luisa:
It's sweet—just like a drama.
Fathers always play the fool.

Huck:
I could speak, if I chose to—

Matt:
Speak what?

Bell:
Shh. Better not.

Huck:
No. I'll be silent.
But you'd better not push it much further.

Matt:
You forget that I'm a hero.
After all, there's my rapier—

Luisa:
And my rape!

Matt:
Ah, what swordplay! Now, that was really living!

Luisa:
That handsome bandit—ah, what hands!
He grabbed me—here!
I've put a little ribbon on the spot.

Matt:
Hot-blooded bandits!
And I cut them down like wheat!

Huck:
I could speak, but I won't.

Bell:
It's tempting, but we shouldn't.

Luisa:
It should be made into an epic poem.

Matt:
I'll write it.

Luisa:
Or better yet—a shrine.

Matt:
Divine! I'll build it.

Luisa:
Where the wall was.

Matt:
This very spot I heard your call,
And here beside our fathers' wall,
I drew my sword and slew them all,
How many—twenty?

Luisa:
Thirty!

Matt:
Yes!—Or even thirty-two
And every one there was to slay,
I slew!

And LUISA swoons in his arms.

Huck:
Ass.

Matt:
I beg your pardon?

75

Huck:

I say that you're an ass!

Matt:

Laughs.

Charming!

Luisa:

Also laughing.

Isn't it? He behaves like a pantaloon!

Huck:

By God, that does it!

Bell:

Wait!

Huck:

No. I'm no pantaloon!
You think that walls come tumbling down?
You think that brigands find an open gate—
The way prepared—You think it's Fate?

Matt:

What do you mean?

Huck:

You think that fathers play the fool
To children barely out of school?

Luisa:

They do in books.

Huck:

In books, maybe.
It's not the same in reality.

No, children——
Children act on puppet stages
Prepared by parents' hard-won wages.
Or do you think such things can be?
You think a First Class Rape comes free!
By God, look at that; it's the villain's fee!

Matt:
What is this?

Bell:
An itemized bill for your pretty little Rape.

Luisa:
But the feud?

Huck:
We arranged it.

Matt:
And the wall?

Bell:
Built to fall.

Matt:
I don't believe it.

Huck:
Read on, Macduff!

Matt:
Reads.

"Item—a silver piece for actor to portray Indian Raiding Party—body paint included."
"Item—a piece in gold to the famous El Gallo for

allowing himself to seem wounded by a beardless, callow boy."

"Item—one moon—"

MATT looks up.

I see you spared no pains.

Luisa:
You mean it wasn't real? The Bandit? The moonlight—?

Matt:
Everything!

Luisa:
But it isn't fair. We didn't need your moon, or bandits. We're in love! We could have made our own moons!

Bell:
Touched.

My child.

Matt:
We were just puppets!

Luisa:
A marriage of convenience!

Bell:
You see. You've spoiled everything!

Huck:
I told you it wouldn't work.

Bell:
You told? *You?* Why, you liar.
Get out of my kumquat!

Huck:

Damn your kumquat!

And HE clips it down to the ground as BELL gasps in horror.

Bell:

That does it! You're a murderer!

Huck:

And you're a fool.

Bell:

Let go of my arm!

Huck:

Stop clipping my hat!

THEY struggle briefly.

Bell:

By God, that does it! I'm going to build up my wall!

Huck:

I too!

Bell:

I'll lime mine up with bottles!

Huck:

I'll jag mine up with glass!

El G:

Comes center to break up the fight.

Pardon me.

Fathers:

Damn!

And THEY exit.

Matt:

Springs up.

Wait!

Luisa:

Oh look! It's my bandit.

Matt:

You are—

Looks at the bill.

El Gallo?

El G:

Sometimes.

Matt:

About this bill. I think you earned it rather easily.

El G:

You made it easy to earn.

Matt:

That's true. But now I will make it harder. Where is my sword! Somebody get me a sword!

El G:

Nice boy.

The MUTE hands MATT a sword.

Matt:

En garde!

El G:

Up a bit with the wrist.

That foot back more.

Aim at the entrails.

That's good—encore!

Thrust One—Thrust Two;
Bend the knee—Thrust Three!
But then be sure to party—
Like this, see.

HE disarms MATT and throws the sword back to the MUTE.

Another lesson?

Matt:
God, I'm a fool!

Luisa:
Always bragging.

Matt:
Don't be sarcastic.

Luisa:
I shall be sarcastic whenever I choose.

Matt:
You think I couldn't do it?

Luisa:
I think you'd better grow up.

Matt:
Grow up! Grow up!
And this from a girl who is sixteen!

Luisa:
Girls mature faster.

Matt:
No. This can't be happening.
If I'm not mad,
If I'm not gloriously insane,

Then I'm just me again.
And if I'm me—
Then I can see.

Luisa:
What?

Matt:
Everything. All the flaws.
You're childish.

Luisa:
Child-like.

Matt:
Silly.

Luisa:
Soulful.

Matt:
And you have freckles!

Luisa:
Suddenly outraged.

That's a lie!

Matt:
I can see them under those pounds of powder.
Look.
Freckles!

Luisa:
I hate you.

Matt:
You see: self-deception. It's a sign of immaturity to
wear lavender perfume before you're forty.

Luisa:
You're a poseur. I've heard you talking in the garden, walking around reciting romantic poems about yourself. He—the bold hero.

Matt:
You're adolescent.

Luisa:
Ahh!

And SHE slaps him. There is a pause. Then as THEY speak, their anger is underscored by music.

Matt:
Beyond that road lies adventure.

Luisa:
I'm going to take my hair down and go swimming in the stream.

Matt:
You'll never hear of me again, my dear. I've decided to be bad.

Luisa:
I'll sit up all night and sing songs to the moon.

Matt:
I'll drink and gamble! I'll grow a moustache. I'll find my madness—somewhere, out there.

Luisa:
I'll find mine too. I'll have an affair!

Matt:
Goodbye forever!

Luisa:
See if I care!

THEY start to leave. EL GALLO snaps his fingers, and THEY stop, frozen in their tracks. EL GALLO takes tear from LUISA's face.

El G:
This tear is enough—this tiny tear.
HE carefully puts it in his pocket....
A boy may go;
The girl must stay.
Thus runs the world away.

Exit LUISA.

MATT is still frozen front, caught in the middle of a dream.

See, he sees it.
And the world seems very grand.

The music has begun, and now MATT sings, as EL GALLO echoes him cynically.

Matt:
Beyond that road lies a shining world.

El G:
Beyond that road lies despair.

Matt:
Beyond that road lies a world that's gleaming—

El G:
People who are scheming.

Matt:
Beauty!

El G:
Hunger.

Matt:
Glory!

El G:
Sorrow.

Matt:
Never a pain or care.

El G:
He's liable to find a couple of surprises there.

Now EL GALLO sings and MATT echoes.

There's a song he must sing;
It's a well-known song
But the tune is bitter
And it doesn't take long to learn.

Matt:
I can learn!

El G:
That pretty little world that beams so bright.
That pretty little world that seems delightful can
burn!

Matt:
Let me learn!
Let me learn!

*And as the tempo picks up, MATT sings of his
vision . .*

For I can see it!
Shining somewhere!
Bright lights somewhere invite me to come there
And learn!
And I'm ready!

I can hear it!
Sirens singing!
Inside my ear I hear them all singing:
Come learn!

Who knows—maybe—
All the visions that I see
May be waiting just for me

To say—take me there, and
Make me see it!
Make me feel it!
I know it's so, I know that it really
May be!
Let me learn!
I can see it!

El G:
He can see it.

Matt:
Shining somewhere!

El G:
Shining somewhere.
Those lights not only glitter, but once there—
They burn!

Matt:
I can hear it!

El G:
He can hear it.

Matt:
Sirens singing!

El G:
Sirens singing.
Don't listen close or maybe you'll never
Return!

Both:
Who knows—may be—
All the visions he (I) can see—
May be waiting just for me
To say—take me there—and

Matt:
Make me see those shining sights inside of me!

El G:
Make him see it!

Matt:
Make me feel those lights inside don't lie to me!

El G:
Make him feel it!

Matt:
I know it's so, I know that it really
May be.
This is what I've always waited for!
This is what my life's created for!

Both:

Let me (him) learn!

El G:

Speaks when the music is over.

The world will teach him
Very quickly
The secret he needs to know.
A certain parable about Romance;
And so—we let him go.
We commit him to the tender mercies
Of that most stringent teacher—Time.
But just so there's no slip-up
We'll add a bit—of spice.

*Enter MORTIMER and HENRY from Prop Box
in stringy wigs and once-colorful disguises.*

Mort:

Hold on there a minute, Matie!

Matt:

What?

Henry:

And where may you be going, my fiery-eyed young
friend? Don't answer; I can see it in your eyes.

Mort:

I see it too— them beady eyes!

Henry:

You go for the goose—the golden goose that lays
the platinum-plated egg, right? Right! I am Lode-

vigo—just like yourself—a young man looking for
the pleasant pinch of adventure.

Matt:
Young man!

Henry:
Yes! And to your left, observe this seamy individu-
al; he is my companion who goes by the name of—
Socrates.

Mort:
I'm Roman.

Henry:
Romanoff, he means. A blue-blood.
He is descended from the Tzars.

Matt:
The Tzars?

Henry:
He is, in fact, the noblest Romanoff of them all.
But enough of chit-chat.

Mort:
Enough. Enough.

Henry:
You long for adventure? We will take you, won't
we, Socci?

Mort:
We'll take him, all right!

Henry:
To the places you've dreamed of—
Venice—Egypt! Ah—Egypt—

"I am dying, Egypt!"—that's a line from something. I don't recall just what.

Matt:
I thought I would—

Henry:
Seek your fortune! Exactly why we're here.
Right, Socci?

Mort:
Right, Loddi. We're going to give you the works!

Henry:
The fireworks, he means.

Matt:
It was my intention—

Henry:
Forget intentions! They paved the road to hell.
We'll see to your education.

Mort:
We know all the ropes!

Henry:
And the ropes to skip, as well!

Mort:
'Eathen idols!

Henry:
Whirling girlies!

Mort:
Tipsy gypsies!

Henry:
Fantastic beauty—just waiting to be unzipped!

Matt:
But I—

Henry:
Clapping his hand over MATT's mouth.

Don't bother to thank us!

Mort:
Doing likewise.

Right! Let's hurry! Loddi—Hurry!

Both:
Singing as THEY up-end him,

Beyond that road—
Is an Episode—
An episode—
An episode—
Beyond that road is an episode—
Look out, you nearly tripped!
Hip. Hip.
Beyond that road is an episode,
An Episode, an episode—
Beyond that road is an episode—
Just waiting to be unzipped!
Hey!

THEY exit carrying MATT.

El G:
Now grant me in your minds a month.
October is over and the sky grows gray.
A month goes by,

91

It's a little bit colder.
A month goes by
We're one month older.

Enter BELLOMY wearing his winter scarf.

Bell:

To MUTE, who is building wall.

That's fine. There's nothing better than a good thick wall. Keep working, friend. Keep working!

HE exits, and HUCKLEBEE comes in on his side. HE sports a winter scarf.

Huck:

Still progressing? Good. We want to get it finished before snowfall.

HE exits, and BELLOMY returns.

Bell:

Hmmm. Getting colder. I'll just take a look at the wall. Fine! Keep on working—Lord, this weather makes a man feel old.

Exit. Enter HUCKLEBEE.

Huck:

Not a word. He's been gone for a month, and I haven't had a single word.

To the MUTE.

How's it going? Hmmm? Oh, I forgot. You're not supposed to talk.

HUCKLEBEE sits in his garden as BELLOMY reappears.

Bell:
Luisa?—Now dear, listen. It's silly to stand in the garden. You'll catch pneumonia. You'll catch asthma. Luisa?

No response.

Well, anyway—I brought you a little shawl.

The FATHERS see each other. THEY hesitate, and then bow gravely. Then THEY stand, face to face, watching the MUTE at work.

Bell:
To the MUTE.

I don't supose you'd care to see my garden?

Huck:
He won't answer.

Bell:
I don't recall addressing that remark to you, sir.

Huck:
He's not supposed to speak.

Bell:
Oh— Oh, well. —By the way . . .

Huck:
Eagerly.

Yes?

Bell:
Oh—nothing.

HUCKLEBEE begins to chuckle.

What's so funny?

Huck:
I was just thinking how we used to meet.

Bell:
Smiles.

Climbing over the wall.

Huck:
Secret meetings—

Bell:
Just to play a little game of cards.

THEY both laugh in delight.
Becoming serious.

How's your son?

Huck:
Not a word.

Bell:
He'll come back— When he runs out of your money.

Huck:
Thank you. And your daughter?

Bell:
Like a statue. Does nothing but dream all day.

Huck:
Pity. —How's your garden?

Bell:
Growing!

Huck:
Mine too.

Bell:
So dependable.
Gardens go on growing.

Huck:
Yes indeed, they do.

Bell:
I tell you, I love vegetables.

Huck:
It's true. I love them too.

And THEY shake hands and sing.

Plant a radish;
Get a radish.
Never any doubt.
That's why I love vegetables;
You know what you're about!

Plant a turnip; get a turnip.
Maybe you'll get two.
That's why I love vegetables;
You know that they'll come through!

They're dependable!
They're befriendable!
They're the best pal a parent's ever known!
While with children—
It's bewilderin'
You don't know until the seed is nearly grown,
Just what you've sown.

So
Plant a carrot,

Get a carrot,
Not a brussel sprout.
That's why I love vegetables,
You know what you're about!

Life is merry,
If it's very
Vegitari—an.
A man who plants a garden
Is a very happy man!

This second chorus THEY sing like a vaudeville team, complete with little awkward dance steps.

Plant a beanstalk;
Get a beanstalk.
Just the same as Jack.
Then if you don't like it,
You can always take it back!

But if your issue
Doesn't kiss you,
Then I wish you luck.
For once you've planted children,
You're absolutely stuck!

Every turnip green!
Every kidney bean!
Every plant grows according to the plot!
While with progeny,
It's hodge-podgenee,
For as soon as you think you know what kind
        you've got,
It's what they're not!

So
Plant a cabbage;
Get a cabbage;
Not a sauerkraut!
That's why I love vegetables!
You know what you're about!

Life is merry
If it's very
Vegitari—an.
A man who plants a garden
Is a very happy man!

He's a vegitari—
Very merry
Vegitari—an!

Bell:

When the song is over.

Say, what about that game of pinochle?

Huck:

I prefer poker.

Bell:

All right, but let's hurry!

Huck:

You still owe me from last time.

To the MUTE.

You keep on working.

Bell:

He's a nice chap.

THEY exit.

LUISA, meanwhile, has begun to come out of her trance.

Luisa:

Oh! Oh! Oh!

Sings.

I'd like to swim in a clear blue stream
Where the water is icy cold.
Then go to town in a golden gown
And have my fortune told.

El G:

Sings.

Just once!
Just once!
Just once before you're old!

Luisa:

It's my bandit!

El G:

Your bandit, yes.

Luisa:

What are you doing up in that tree?

El G:

Growing ripe.

Luisa:

Don't grow too ripe or you'll fall.

El G:

Very wise.

Luisa:
What do you see from up there?

El G:
Everything.

Luisa:
Really?

El G:
Nearly.

Luisa:
Do you see Matt?

El G:
Do you care?

Luisa:
No, I just wondered.
Can I climb up there beside you?

El G:
You can if you can.

Luisa:
Joins him.

There!
I don't see everything.

El G:
It takes a little while.

Luisa:
All I see is my own house. And Matt's.
And the wall.

El G:
And that's all?

Luisa:

All.
Is it fun to be a bandit?

El G:

It has its moments.

Luisa:

I think it must be fun.
Tell me,
Do you ride on a great white horse?

El G:

I used to.

Luisa:

But no longer?

El G:

I developed a saddle rash.
Very painful.

Luisa:

How unglamorous.
I never heard of a hero
Who had a saddle rash.

El G:

Oh, it happens. Occupational hazard.

Luisa:

Tell me,
What is your favourite plunder?

El G:

Plunder?
I think that's Pirates.

Luisa:
Well then, booty.

El G:
You've been reading too many books.

Luisa:
Well, you must steal *something!*

El G:
I steal fancies. I steal whatever is treasured most.

Luisa:
That's more like it—
Precious rubies!

El G:
Looking at her necklace.

Precious rhinestones.

Luisa:
Rhinestones?

El G:
Can be precious.
It depends on the point of view.

Luisa:
Well, it doesn't sound very sound.
Economically, I mean.

El G:
Pretty child.

Luisa:
Do you think so?
Do I attract you?

El G:
Somewhat.

Luisa:
Oh, that's splendid!
Look, see this ribbon.
That's where you gave me a bruise.

El G:
I'm so sorry.

Luisa:
Don't be silly. I adore it!
I kiss it three times every day.
Tell me,
Have you seen the world?

El G:
A bit, yes.

Luisa:
Is it like in the books?

El G:
Depends on which books you read.

Luisa:
The adventures. The Romances.
"Cast off thy name.
A rose by any other name—"
Do you know that?

El G:
Sounds familiar.

Luisa:
"Put up thy sword. The dew will rust it!"

That's Othello. He was older than Desdemona,
But she loved him because he had seen the world.
Of course he killed her.

El G:
Of course.

Luisa:
"It's a far better thing that I do now
Than I have ever done before!"
Isn't that beautiful? That man was beheaded.

El G:
I'm not surprised.

Luisa:
Take me there!

El G:
Where?

Luisa:
To the parties! To the world!

El G:
But I'm a bandit.
There is a price upon my head.

Luisa:
Oh. I was hoping that there would be!

El G:
You and I!
Us together!

Luisa:
Yes. Dancing forever and forever!

El G:

Sings.

Round and round
Till the break of day.
Candles glow,
Fiddles play,
Why not be wild if we feel that way?
Reckless and terrible gay!

Round and round,
'Neath a magic spell.
Velvet gown,
Pink lapel.
Life is a colorful carousel.
Reckless and terribly gay!

Luisa:

I'm ready anytime,
If you'll take me, I'm
Ready to go!
So show the way to me,
I will try to be,
Ready to go!

El G:

I seem to see Venice,
We're on a lagoon.
A gondolier's crooning
A gondola tune.
The air makes your hair billow blue in the moon.

Luisa:

I could swoon!

El G:
You're so blue in the moon!

And now THEY begin to dance. The MUTE hands her a mask—a paper mask of a blank face; a laughing-hollow mask; a stylish face that is frozen forever into unutterable joy. This mask is upon a little hand-stick—so that when held in front of one's visage, it blocks out any little tell-tale traces of compassion or of horror.

As LUISA and El GALLO go on dancing, we see —in a stylized blaze of light—MORTIMER and HENRY up on the platform stage—waving "flames" of torn red silk. At first THEY are gondoliers—but as the action gets wilder, THEY change into rioting peasants. In each of these sequences, it is MATT who is the object of their fury.

Luisa:
Spoken.
Look at the peasants.
They're lighting candelabras.
No, I believe they're lighting torches.
Yes, see—
They've started burning the palaces.
—There goes the Doge!

Henry:
A rivederci!

Luisa:
Oh, what fun!

I *adore* pyrotechnics!

Suddenly MORTIMER and HENRY set MATT on fire.

Luisa:
That man—look out; he's burning.
My God, he's on fire!

El G:
Keep on dancing.

Luisa:
But he's burning—

El G:
Just put up your mask—
Then it's pretty.

Matt:
Help! Help!

EL GALLO raises the mask to her face.

Luisa:
Oh yes, isn't he *beautiful!*
He's all sort of orange.
Red-orange.
That's one of my favorite colors!

Matt:
Help!

Luisa:
You look lovely!

MORTIMER and HENRY pull MATT down and out of sight as the MUTE holds up a silk cloth to shield them—the effect being rather like a Punch and Judy show that is being performed on the platform.

El G:

As LUISA sings a wild obligato.

We'll just
Dance!
We'll kick up our heels to music.
And dance!
Until my head reels with music
Like a lovely real romance,
All we'll do is daily dance.
All we'll do is just dance.
All we'll do is just dance.
All we'll do is just—

Luisa:

Speaks.

Whee. I'm exhausted.

El G:

Speaks.

But you can't be.
The evening's just started!

MUSIC. As HE starts singing again.

Round and round
Till the break of day.
Candles glow.
Fiddles play.
Why not be wild if we feel that way.
Reckless and terribly gay!

Luisa:

> I'm ready anytime,
> If you'll take me, I'm
> Ready to go!
> So show the way to me,
> I will try to be,
> Ready to go!

El G:

> I seem to see Athens, it's terribly chic.
> Atop the Acropolis, it's terribly Greek.
> There's Venus, Adonis, 'n us—cheek to cheek.

Luisa:

> Oh how chic!

El G:

> To be Greek cheek to cheek!

> *Once more we see MORTIMER and HENRY in
> colorful attire. And once more MATT is along
> with them. HE is ragged and disheveled—and HE
> is much the worse for wear.*

Luisa:

> *Speaks.*

> Observe the friendly natives!
> La, how gay.
> Look dear, they're beating a monkey.
> Isn't that fun.
> I wonder why anyone should be beating a monkey?
> Oh no, that's it.
> It's not a monkey at all.

It's a man dressed in a monkey suit.
That man—they've hurt him!

El G:
Put up the mask.

Luisa:
But he is wounded.

El G:
The Mask! The Mask!

Matt:
Help!

And once more EL GALLO presses the sophisticated mask up to her face.

Luisa:
Oh, isn't that cute.
They're beating a man in a monkey suit.
It's a show. La, how jolly.
Don't stop; it's charming.
Don't stop.

Matt:
Help!

Luisa:
That's it. Writhe some more.

And the "puppets" disappear again, as the MUTE holds up the cloth in front of them.

El G:
We'll just
Dance!

We'll kick up our heels to music
And dance!
Until my head reels with music
Like a lovely real romance.
All we'll do is daily dance.
All we'll do is just dance.
All we'll do is just dance.
All we'll do is just—

Luisa:
Speaks.

Couldn't we just sit this one out?

El G:
Speaks.

Ridiculous! When there's music to be danced to?
Play gypsies!

Both:
Round and round
'Neath a magic spell.
Velvet gown,
Pink lapel.
Life is a colorful carousel.
Reckless and terribly gay.

Luisa:
I'm ready anytime.
If you'll take me, I'm
Ready to go!
So show the way to me,
I will try to be,
Ready to go!

El G:

We'll be in Bengazi or maybe Bombay.
I understand Indja is terribly gay.
The natives assemble on feast day and play

Luisa:

With their snakes?

El G:

What a racket it makes!

Luisa:

Speaks.

I think I'm going to love Indja.
Such a big population, and
I adore crowds!
Oh look, there's a fakir—
Hi, Fakir!

Henry:

A bit confused.

A rivederci!

Luisa:

See—he's there with his assistants.
They all know Yogi—
And they're just loads of fun!
There's one—a young one—
They're putting him down on some nails.

SHE puts down her mask.

If he fails,
He'll be cut to bits by those nails.

Matt:
Help!

Luisa:
Someone help him.

El G:
The mask!

Luisa:
But he's bleeding!

El G:
Mask!

Luisa:
Horrible!

El G:
Mask!

And HE forces it up to her face. Once more, the transition.

Luisa:
Go on. Sit down harder.
He's a sissy.
I don't believe he's a real fakir.
They never complain.
He's a fake fakir.

Matt:
Help!

Luisa:
Fake!

All:
Sing.

We'll—
Just—
Dance—!
We'll kick up our heels to music
And dance!
Until my head reels with music.
Like a lovely real romance,
All we'll do is daily
    I can see the friendly natives!
All we'll do is just dance.
All we'll do is just dance.
All we'll do is just—
Round and round in a magic spell.
All we'll do is just;
All we'll do is just;
All we'll do is just—
Dance!

*At the end of the number, HENRY, MOR-
TIMER, and MATT have gone, and LUISA and
EL GALLO are back in the tree, exactly like the
scene before.*

El G:

Now hurry. You must pack so that we may run
away.

Luisa:

Kiss me first.

El G:

All right.

Luisa:

Ahh.

El G:

What is it?

Luisa:

At last! I have been kissed upon the eyes. No matter what happens, I'll never never ever forget that kiss. I'll go now.

El G:

One word, Luisa, listen:
I want to tell you this—
I promise to remember too
That one particular kiss.
. . . And now hurry; we have a lifetime for kisses.

Luisa:

True. You'll wait here?

El G:

I promise.

Luisa:

All right then.

El G:

Wait. Give me a trinket—to pledge that you will come back. That necklace—

Luisa:

Was my Mother's.

El G:

Good. It will serve as your pledge.

Luisa:

All right. I leave you this necklace because it is my favourite thing. Here, guard it. I won't be long.

SHE starts to go and then turns back.

It's really like that? The world is like you say?

El G:

Of course.

Sings.

"Beyond that road lies a shining world."

And suddenly we see MATT returning. HE is in shadow, and neither LUISA nor EL GALLO take any notice of HIM as HE sings:

Matt:

Beyond that road lies despair.

El G:

Beyond that road lies a world that's gleaming.

Matt:

People who are scheming.

El G:

Beauty!

Matt:

Hunger!

El G:

Glory!

Matt:

Sorrow!

El G:

With never a pain or care.

Matt:
She's liable to find a couple of surprises there.

Luisa:
I'm ready. I won't be long.

Once more, SHE turns back.

You will be here?

El G:
Right here. I promise.

When LUISA has gone, EL GALLO turns to leave. He is interrupted by MATT.

Matt:
Wait.

El G:
Well, The Prodigal Son comes home.

Matt:
Don't leave her like that.
It isn't fair.

El G:
It's her misfortune,
What do you care?

Matt:
She's too young.
I said, don't leave her!

MATT tries to stop him. EL GALLO raises his hand and hits the BOY, knocking him down to his knees, then EL GALLO moves into the shadows at the side.

LUISA returns. SHE calls out for EL GALLO, but HE isn't there. SHE continues to call his name as SHE begins to realize that SHE has been left. Then slowly SHE sinks to her knees, on the opposite side of the stage from MATT. EL GALLO appears from the shadows and addresses the audience.

El G:
> There is a curious paradox
> That no one can explain.
> Who understands the secret
> Of the reaping of the grain?
>
> Who understands why Spring is born
> Out of Winter's laboring pain?
> Or why we all must die a bit
> Before we grow again.
>
> I do not know the answer.
> I merely know it's true.
> I hurt them for that reason
> And myself a little bit too.

HE steps back into the shadows.

Matt:
> It isn't worth tears, believe me.
> Luisa, please—don't cry.

Luisa:
> You look awful.

Matt:
> I know.

Luisa:
    What's that swelling?

Matt:
    That's my eye.

Luisa:
    Oh. And those scratches.
    What in the world happened to you?

Matt:
    The world happened to me.

Luisa:
    Did you drink and gamble?

Matt:
    The first day, yes.
    But the drink was drugged,
    And the wheel kept hitting sixes.
    Until I played a six.

Luisa:
    Did you serenade señoras?

Matt:
    I did for a little while.
    Until I got hit.

Luisa:
    Hit?

Matt:
    With a slop pot.

Luisa:
    What?

Matt:

    A Spanish slop pot.

    Believe me, it defies description.

Luisa:

    Smiles.

    I'm sorry, Matt.

Matt:

    No. It's all right. I deserve it.

    I've been foolish.

Luisa:

    I have too. Believe me.

    More than you.

    And simply—very simply—THEY face each other and sing:

Matt:

    When the moon was young,

    When the month was May,

    When the stage was hung for my holiday,

    I saw shining lights, but I never knew—

    They were you

    They were you

    They were you.

Luisa:

    When the dance was done,

    When I went my way,

    When I tried to find rainbows far away,

    All the lovely lights seemed to fade from view—

    They were you

They were you
They were you.

Both:

Without you near me,
I can't see.
When you're near me.
Wonderful things come to be.
Every secret prayer,
Every fancy free,
Every thing I dared for both you and me,
All my wildest dreams multiplied by two,
They were you
They were you
They were you.

Luisa:

I missed you, Matt.

Matt:

I missed you too.

Luisa:

Oh, you've been hurt.

Matt:

Yes.

Luisa:

But you should have told me.
You should have told me that right away.
Here, sit down. Maybe I can bind it.

THEY sit on the platform, as the MUTE stands

above and behind them and sprinkles them with paper "snow."

Matt:
You've been hurt, too.

Luisa:
Yes.

Matt:
It's beginning to snow.

Luisa:
I know.

Matt:
Here. Take my coat.

Luisa:
No. Both.
There's room enough for both.

THEY pull close together and THEY sing.

Both:
Love.
You are love. (You are love.)
Better far than a metaphor can ever, ever be.
Love—You are love. (You are love.)
My mystery— (My mystery)
of Love—

And the FATHERS, who have been sitting up-stage, now rise and come forward.

Bell:
Look!

El G:

Who has watched it all, steps forward.

Shh.

Huck:
They've come back.

Bell:
It's a miracle. Let's take down the wall.

El G:
No. Leave the wall.
Remember—
You must always leave the wall.

Sings, as the others hum beneath him.

Deep in December, it's nice to remember,
Although you know the snow will follow.
Deep in December, it's nice to remember:
Without a hurt the heart is hollow.

Deep in December, it's nice to remember
The fire of September that made us mellow.
Deep in December, our hearts should remember
And follow.

*And the MUTE gets the "FANTASTICKS" drape
from the prop box. And HE and EL GALLO carefully hang it on the poles in front of the PAR-
ENTS and the LOVERS. And when the stage, in
fact, is as it was in the beginning, the lights dim
down. And the play, of course, is done.*

BARD BOOKS
DISTINGUISHED DRAMA

BENT, Martin Sherman ....75754-0/$2.50
BIZARRE BEHAVIOR: SIX PLAYS BY
INNAURATO, Albert Innaurato ....75903-9/$3.50
EQUUS, Peter Shaffer ....51797-3/$2.50
FANTASTICKS, Jones Schmidt .... 54007-X/$2.50
GAY PLAYS: THE FIRST COLLECTION
William H. Hoffman, Ed. ....77263-9/$3.95
GETTING OUT, Marsha Norman............75184-4/$2.50
GREAT JEWISH PLAYS, Joseph C. Landis ....51573-3/$3.50
HISTORY OF THE AMERICAN FILM
Christopher Durang ....39271-2/$1.95
THE IMPORTANCE OF BEING EARNEST
Oscar Wilde................................77404-6/$1.95
KEY EXCHANGE, Kevin Wade ....61119-8/$2.50
MASS APPEAL, Bill C. Davis ....77396-1/$2.50
MEMOIR, John Murrell .... 38521-X/$1.95
MISS MARGARIDA'S WAY
Roberto Athayde ....40568-7/$1.95
PETER PAN, OR THE BOY WHO WOULD NOT
GROW UP, James M. Barrie ....57752-6/$2.95
PIPPIN,
Roger O. Hirson & Stephen Schwartz ....45740-7/$2.25
THE RING: FOUR PLAYS FOR CHILDREN
Adapted by Philip Caggiano...................79434-9/$2.50
RUNNER STUMBLES, Milan Stitt ....44719-3/$2.25
TOAD OF TOAD HALL, A.A. Milne ....58115-9/$2.95
UNCOMMON WOMEN AND OTHERS
Wendy Wasserstein ....80580-4/$2.95
WAKEFIELD PLAY'S, Israel Horovitz.........42903-9/$3.50
WHOSE LIFE IS IT ANYWAY?, Brian Clark... 64808-3/$2.95

NEW FROM AVON ✪BARD
DISTINGUISHED
MODERN FICTION

DR. RAT   63990-4/$3.95
William Kotzwinkle
This chilling fable by the bestselling author of THE FAN MAN and FATA MORGANA is an unforgettable indictment of man's inhumanity to man, and to all living things. With macabre humor and bitter irony, Kotzwinkle uses Dr. Rat as mankind's apologist in an animal experimentation laboratory grotesquely similar to a Nazi concentration camp.

ON THE WAY HOME   63131-8/$3.50
Robert Bausch
This is the powerful, deeply personal story of a man who came home from Vietnam and what happened to his family.
"A strong, spare, sad and beautiful novel, exactly what Hemingway should write, I think, if he'd lived through the kind of war we make now."   John Gardner
"A brilliant psychological study of an intelligent, close family in which something has gone terribly and irretrievably wrong."   *San Francisco Chronicle*

AGAINST THE STREAM   63693-X/$4.95
James Hanley
"James Hanley is a most remarkable writer....Beneath this book's calm flow there is such devastating emotion."
The New York Times Book Review
This is the haunting, illuminating novel of a young child whose arrival at the isolated stone mansion of his mother's family unleashes their hidden emotions and forces him to make a devastating choice.

NEW FROM  AVON BARD

DISTINGUISHED MODERN FICTION

SENT FOR YOU YESTERDAY
John Edgar Wideman   82644-5/$3.50
In SENT FOR YOU YESTERDAY, John Edgar Wideman, "one of America's premier writers of fiction" (*The New York Times*), tells the passion of ordinary lives, the contradictions, perils, pain and love which are the blood and bone of everybody's America. "Perhaps the most gifted black novelist in his generation." *The Nation*

Also from Avon Bard: **DAMBALLAH** (78519-6/$2.95) and
HIDING PLACE (78501-3/$2.95)

THE LEOPARD'S TOOTH
William Kotzwinkle   62869-4/$2.95
A supernatural tale of a turn-of-the-century archaeological expedition to Africa and the members' breathtaking adventures with the forces of good and evil, by "one of today's most inventive writers." (Playboy).

DREAM CHILDREN
Gail Godwin   62406-0/$3.50
Gail Godwin, the bestselling author of A MOTHER AND TWO DAUGHTERS (61598-3/$3.95), presents piercing, moving, beautifully wrought fiction about women possessed of imagination, fantasy, vision and obsession who live within the labyrinths of their minds. "Godwin is a writer of enormous intelligence, wit and compassion...DREAM CHILDREN is a fine place to start catching up with an extraordinary writer." *Saturday Review*

Available wherever paperbacks are sold or directly from the publisher. Include $1.00 per copy for postage and handling: allow 6-8 weeks for delivery. Avon Books, Dept BP, Box 767, Rte 2, Dresden, TN 38225.